IMAGES
of America

DELAWARE IN
WORLD WAR II

IMAGES
of America

DELAWARE IN
WORLD WAR II

Peter F. Slavin and Timothy A. Slavin

ARCADIA
PUBLISHING

Published by Arcadia Publishing
Charleston, South Carolina

Printed in the United States of America

Library of Congress Catalog Card Number: 2004101850

For all general information contact Arcadia Publishing at:
Telephone 843-853-2070
Fax 843-853-0044
E-mail sales@arcadiapublishing.com
For customer service and orders:
Toll-Free 1-888-313-2665

Visit us on the Internet at www.arcadiapublishing.com

CONTENTS

ACKNOWLEDGMENTS

Our thanks to those who helped in this small volume of history extend across three generations.

Delaware is home to one of the finest archival facilities and programs in the world, and the collections of the Delaware Public Archives are an untapped vein of gold for the historian of World War II. Former State Archivist Leon deValinger Jr., with unmatched foresight and vision, collected the myriad records of war activities as events happened. The resulting collection is rich not only with the photographs in this volume, but with clippings, letters, handbills, ration cards, and other memorabilia. We owe a debt of gratitude to that vision; DeValinger's legacy to Delaware will continue to be felt for generations to come.

In 1955, deValinger and William H. Conner published the two-volume *Delaware's Role in World War II*, which serves as the seminal work about Delaware's role in the war. It was reprinted by the Delaware Heritage Commission in 2003, and now a new generation of scholars and historians have access to this important work.

Our thanks also go to the staff of the Delaware Public Archives for continuing a long and proud tradition of preserving the state's history, while also making it readily and easily available to the researcher. Special thanks go to those who assist the researcher—Heather Jones, Dawn Mitchell, Cynthia Caldwell, Michelle Peterson, Terence Burns, Valda Perry, and Chris Burns; those who preserve the archives—Joanne Mattern, Randy Goss, and Bruce Haase; and those who help to create new ways of using these important records—Tom Summers and Lori Hatch.

The photographs in this volume also provided an unforeseen benefit—they allowed three generations of our family to help preserve our own family's history. We benefited from the research of a younger generation—Esa Slavin, age 16 and Jack Knox, age 13—whose interest in their country's history was matched by the effect it had on their own family. We also benefited greatly from the insight, interest, and undying support our father, Joseph F. Slavin, brought to the project. Sparked by each photograph, his remembrances of events and conversations now serve as one family's archive of World War II in the Slavin home.

We dedicate this book to our father, Joseph F. Slavin. Like many of his generation—too young to enlist, but not too young to help—he watched others go before him. His own brothers, John and Edward, left their young brother, put on the uniform of their country, and by the grace of God, returned to tell the story. In their absence, our Dad—like so many others on the home front in World War II and so many others in this book—accepted his new role with maturity far beyond his years.

Thanks for making history, Dad.

Peter F. Slavin
Timothy A. Slavin

INTRODUCTION

Delaware's response to World War II is often measured in ways that are tangible and understood: more than 33,000 servicemen and women in uniform as of 1945, young men lined up around the block at a Wilmington recruiting office on the day after Pearl Harbor, and, most importantly, the Delawareans who gave their life for the cause of war.

Delawareans on the home front faced challenges that, while not as dire as combat, were certainly no less important in the story of World War II.

The home front—the war's forgotten theater—provides a rich and complex history of a society completely remade by the onset of a global conflict. From urban factories to rural farms, every part of Delaware felt the effects of the war. And every citizen of Delaware did their share.

This history tells the story of Delaware in World War II. It intends to show how every corner of the state responded to the war, how individual citizens changed their lives, and how their lives were changed forever.

The home front in Delaware was a busy place. Factories like Pusey and Jones, Dravo Shipyards, and Bellanca Aviation not only re-tooled to produce war materials, but also added shifts to meet demand. Women entered the work force in large numbers for the first time, in large part to make up for the shortage of workers. Farmers in Kent and Sussex Counties grew crops in records numbers and relied on an all-out effort from volunteers, school children, stateside soldiers, and even prisoners-of-war to harvest their crops without loss. Children took on new responsibility, heading up scrap drives to collect unwanted metal or paper.

While many of the names of individuals in the photos have been lost to history, many individual stories remain. Mrs. Clem Gale of Wilmington was dubbed the "heroine of the Delaware Salvage Drive" for collecting 12,088 tin cans. Daphne Powell, a student at Bayard Junior High School, collected more than 1,000 unwanted keys, earning her top honors. Henry Stewart of Centerville drove a salvage truck more than 10,000 hours, logging more than 50,000 miles across the state.

Through all these stories, one theme is prevalent: Delaware was united in the cause. This is apparent in many of the slogans and posters which encouraged home front participation: "We Need You Now" was used to recruit civilians into defense-related jobs; "Will You Help?" was the recruiting cry from the Red Cross; "It's My Fight Too" encouraged women to buy war bonds; and even the somewhat whimsical "Candy is Fighting Food" was used by the USO to help our men and women in uniform.

The history of Delaware in World War II, replete with the many home front activities, is a piece of our heritage. Let us preserve that story with the same determination with which it was made.

One

"WE NEED YOU NOW"
Civilians in the Workplace

WE NEED YOU NOW. As
the war effort grew, many
home front industries were
in need of new workers.
Existing jobs became
available when citizens
enlisted and were deployed,
and industries re-tooled
their production to support
the war effort. A recruiting
drive such as this, in
which the Civil Service
Commission sponsored
tours of a military
airplane, helped to attract
civilians to such openings.
(Delaware Public Archives,
1325.205, Box 1.)

MAKING PLANES, BELLANCA AIRCRAFT. With the outbreak of the war, New Castle–based Bellanca Aircraft re-tooled its operations from the manufacturing of commercial aircraft to making components that supported the war effort. The company would run two separate production shifts, keeping their manufacturing factory staffed for 20 hours a day. Bellanca employed many women in these shifts to cover the demand for its product. See Chapter Three for images of women at work at Bellanca. (Delaware Public Archives, 1325.206, 2078.)

GUN TURRETS, BELLANCA AIRCRAFT. Bellanca specialized in making the Martin Gun Turret, which was used in bombing and training planes, tanks, and PT boats. (Delaware Public Archives, 1325.206, 2086.)

MOULDING GANG AT EASTERN MALLEABLE. A moulding gang at the Eastern Malleable Iron Company in Wilmington is shown making truck parts. The company manufactured low carbon steel. At the height of its production, the company produced 825 tons of castings with a labor force of 500. (Delaware Public Archives, 1325.205, Box 1.)

POURING GANG. This photograph of a pouring gang at Eastern Malleable depicts some of the difficult work the company completed. Working in high temperatures and with dangerous materials, the men and women of the company worked long hours to meet the demand. Eventually, a labor shortage resulted in the company scaling back its operations. (Delaware Public Archives, 1325.206, 2264.)

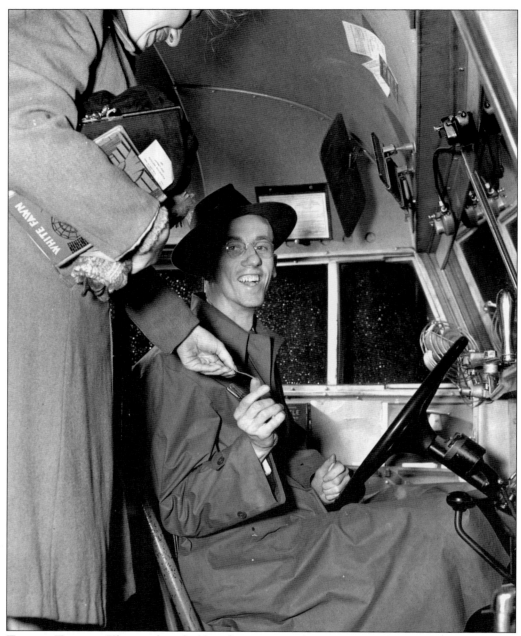

TAKING TICKETS. This unidentified bus driver was, in fact, a minister from Bellefonte, who did his part by driving a bus during wartime. Many stateside civilians changed their lives to take on new roles in Delaware. (Delaware Public Archives, 1325.206, 2294.)

STILL CONDUCTING. D.J. Truitt, a conductor on the Delmarva Express passenger rail service, supported the war efforts by continuing to take tickets, even at the age of 70. Passenger rail service was one of the primary means of transporting troops that were stationed stateside; some of the uniformed men appear in the foreground of this photograph. (Delaware Public Archives, 1325.206, 2251.)

BAGGAGE CAR. With the increase in demand for wartime travel, passengers on this Wilmington-to-Dover train were forced to travel inside a baggage car for the trip. More than 180 passengers could fit in such a car, but had to spend the entire trip either standing, or sitting on their luggage. (Delaware Public Archives, 1325.205, Box 1.)

DuPont Supports the War.
The plastics department of the
DuPont Company was responsible
for manufacturing Lucite noses
for the Martin Bomber. DuPont
would support the war effort with
an almost complete re-engineering
of its plants; its 1941 annual report
would boast that more than half of
its production was for war-related
goods. (Delaware Public Archives,
1325.206, 2194.)

Feeding the Troops. One of
the areas of DuPont's involvement
was the manufacture of ready-
to-eat meals for servicemen and
women. (Delaware Public Archives,
1325.206, 2206.)

CHINESE WORKERS AT DRAVO SHIPYARDS. Dravo Shipyards in Wilmington produced destroyer escorts, patrol crafts, and dredges. At the height of its production, the company was forced to use overseas labor. These recently arrived Chinese workers are shown getting a quick lesson in English. (Delaware Public Archives, 1325.206, 2151.)

SUB CHASER. The PC 578 was a submarine chaser built by Dravo Shipyards. This chaser is shown on its inaugural run, after being placed in service on September 2, 1942. (Delaware Public Archives, 1325.206, 2161.)

LAUNCHING OF THE SENEGALAIS, NOVEMBER 11, 1943. This ceremony marked the launch of the *Senegalais*, a destroyer escort, at the Dravo Shipyard in Wilmington. Vice Admiral Raymond Fenard, head of the French Naval Mission, is shown speaking. The crew of the *Senegalais* would be honored later in the war for sinking a German U-boat. (Delaware Public Archives, 1325.206, 2154.)

DRAVO IN ACTION. British equipment disembarks a Dravo-built landing ship transport in the English Channel during the D-Day invasion of Normandy, France in June 1944. (Delaware Public Archives, 1325.205, Box 1.)

THE M-51. The M-51 Multiple Machine Gun is shown here on display as part of a war bond rally. The M-51 included many components manufactured in Delaware, including the gun turret. It was common for such Delaware-made components to be highlighted in war bond rallies. (Delaware Public Archives, 1325.206, 1793.)

EMERGENCY HOUSING, NEWARK. Delaware's builders joined the war efforts by building emergency housing for servicemen and workers who were brought to the area. These houses were part of the George Read Village in Newark. (Delaware Public Archives, 1325.206, 2040.)

EASTLAKE. This vacant lot at the corner of North Locust Street and East 26th Street in Wilmington was chosen as the site for the Eastlake Housing Community. It was one of several federal housing projects in Wilmington, and federal funds were used to operate nursery schools at the sites, so that mothers could enter the workforce. (Delaware Public Archives, 1325.206, 2029.)

SOUTHBRIDGE. Officials break ground at the Southbridge Housing Community, another emergency housing community created during the war effort. (Delaware Public Archives, 1325.206, 2035.)

MILLSIDE. The dedication of Millside, another wartime housing development, took place in Wilmington on October 1, 1943. The development was initiated with funding from the Federal Public Housing Authority. (Delaware Public Archives, 1325.205, Box 1.)

DEDICATION OF EASTLAKE. The dedication of the Eastlake Community was a milestone for the City of Wilmington—it was the first city to open subsidized nursery schools under the Lanham Act. The nursery school at Eastlake was open from 6:30 a.m. to 6:30 p.m.; families paid $3 per child per week, which included lunch. (Delaware Public Archives, 1325.206, 2027.)

ENJOYING EASTLAKE. One of the benefits of the housing communities was the common recreational area offered to children. (Delaware Public Archives, 1325.206, 2024.)

Two

"BLOCK OUT THIS MENACE"
Raising Money for the War Effort

BLOCK OUT THIS MENACE.
Delawareans were generous
in their financial support of
the war and benefited from
numerous clever campaigns.
The United War Fund of
Delaware had a goal to raise
$900,000; for every $10,000
contributed one block of
Adolf Hitler's face would
be blocked out. The sign
remained in a prominent
location in Wilmington as a
subtle reminder of the need to
raise money for the war effort.
(Delaware Public Archives,
1325.206, 2553.)

THE MENACE IS BLOCKED OUT. On November 23, 1943, the General War Fund reached its goal of raising $900,000 and put the final block over the image of Adolf Hitler. (Delaware Public Archives, 1325.206, 2554.)

PUSEY & JONES. Rallies such as this one on the floor of Pusey & Jones were part thank-you and part fund-raiser. The men and women workers at the shipyard were given time to enjoy the music, while also signing up to purchase war bonds. (Delaware Public Archives, 1325.206, 2232-2254.)

EDGEMOOR IRON WORKS. Another common occurrence was to have servicemen on leave return to their home city and make appeals directly to workers, such as here at the Edgemoor Iron Works. Pacific theater veterans—standing in the booth on the left—appealed for more bonds to be purchased. Those on the speakers stand include (left to right) William B. Stormfeltz, Machinist Mate D.H. Dillon, General Foreman David Riley, Electricians Mate K.P. Nelson, General Manager C.E. Thompson, and Donald Kemp and Harry Gray of the company. (Delaware Public Archives, 1325. 206, 2264.)

GOVERNOR BACON SELLS A BOND. Gov. Walter Bacon sells the first bond for the Fifth War Loan drive in June 1944. Delawareans exceeded the goal for war loan drives, buying more than $500 million worth of bonds. (Delaware Public Archives, 1325.206, Box 1.)

RIDE THE CYCLOPS. The Seventh War Loan Drive included new slogans and incentives to buy war bonds. Claiming that citizens could "strike a blow at Tokyo" by buying a war bond, the Delaware Trust Company offered a free ride in the "Cyclops" for any investor purchasing a $100 war bond. (Delaware Public Archives, 1325.206, 1719.)

BUYING AT BELLANCA. A war bond rally at the Bellanca Air Company field included a patriotic band (just below the stage) and a sign that read "People United for Victory, Parts United for Victory." (Delaware Public Archives, 1325.206, 2124.)

DROWN THE RAT. For the Fourth War Loan Drive, this airman helped the effort with his artistic depiction of a rat-like Adolf Hitler being drowned in a sea of war bonds. The drive was successful in reaching its goal of $350,000. (Delaware Public Archives, 1325.206, 479.)

WE CAN'T ALL GO, BUT WE CAN PAY THE FARE. This crossroads sign was erected in 1943 as part of the 2nd War Loan drive and included mileage from Wilmington to both Tokyo (6,746 miles) and Berlin (1,968 miles). The sign also included the slogan "We can't all go, but we can pay the fare of our fighting boys." (Delaware Public Archives, 1325.206, 1623.)

DANCE TO THE JIVE BOMBERS. A military band, the Jive Bombers, entertain Wilmingtonians during a free outdoor concert to promote war bonds during the Third War Loan drive. (Delaware Public Archives, 1325.206, 475.)

JAPANESE SUB ON DOVER'S GREEN. A captured Japanese submarine was towed into Dover and put on exhibition on Dover's Green to publicize a war bond drive. The crowds that gathered to see this were among the largest for any war bond rally held in Dover. (Delaware Public Archives, 1325.205, Box 1.)

PARADING DOWN LOOCKERMAN STREET. Numerous units from the Dover Army Airbase paraded down Loockerman Street in the heart of Dover to help raise funds for the Third War Loan Drive in October 1942. (Delaware Public Archives, 1325.206, 1614–1641.)

MARCHING PAST DOVER CITY HALL. Troops from the Dover Army Airbase march past the old Dover City Hall (in background) on their way down Loockerman Street. (Delaware Public Archives, 1325.206, 141.)

CAPTURED SUB RAISES FUNDS. A captured German submarine arrived in Wilmington as part of the United War Fund drive. The new commander of the submarine was Lt. H.D. Mann. From left to right are L.A. Webster, State War Fund director; J.B. Fulenwider, chairman of the United War Fund Committee; machinist R.D. Reynolds; Lt. H.D. Mann; Ensign D.P. Schaunberg; and Charles Petze. (Delaware Public Archives, 1325.206, 2555.)

HE'S UP TO HIS NECK. Funds that were raised by a waste paper salvage drive are presented as part of the effort for the United War Fund. Delaware's goal of raising $823,500 was met, thanks to efforts like these and posters like that in the background, which reads, "He's up to his neck, too but he's giving back." (Delaware Public Archives, 1325.206, 2558.)

R.I.P. SOUTH YARD. Workers commemorate the end of the war bond drives with a symbolic burial in 1945. (Delaware Public Archives, 1325.206, 2268.)

Three

"ARE YOU A GIRL WITH A STAR-SPANGLED HEART?"
Women in Support of the War

ARE YOU A GIRL WITH A STAR-SPANGLED HEART? When President Franklin Delano Roosevelt signed a law in 1941 creating the Women's Army Corps (WACs), women other than nurses were allowed to serve within the Army. More than 150,000 women would serve the country in the WACs. These early WAC recruits in a Wilmington recruiting office were enticed with a recruiting poster (on the back wall), which asked "Are you a girl with a star-spangled heart?" (Delaware Public Archives, 1325.206, 948-973.)

SIGNING UP. These WAC recruits joined the service in 1944, signing their papers against a backdrop of what a typical WAC's day might look like at the New Castle Army Air Base. (Delaware Public Archives, 1325.205, Box 1 chapter 15.)

NEWLY RECRUITED MEMBERS OF THE WAVES. Women Accepted for Volunteer Emergency Service in the United States Navy board a bus to Hunter College for training. WAVES performed clerical and secretarial functions in the Navy to free up more men for fighting. (Delaware Public Archives, 1325.205, box 1 chapter 15.)

ENLISTING THE WACS. One of the first group of women enlisting in the WACs in Delaware are sworn into the service in the office of Wilmington Mayor James. (Delaware Public Archives, 1325.205, box 1 chapter 15.)

WASPS IN UNIFORM. The Womens Airforce Service Pilots, or WASPs, were responsible for providing ferrying service for aircraft during the war. The service was initiated in October 1942 with an all-women flight of six pilots ferrying six liaison aircraft to Mitchel Field in New York from Lock Haven, Pennsylvania. The WASPs, with a strong contingent at the New Castle Army Airbase, eventually totaled more than 1,000 members before being deactivated in December 1944. (Delaware Public Archives, 1325.205, box 1 chapter 3.)

MILK PARTY. WACs enjoy some down time with a milk party at the New Castle Army Airbase. The WACs were eligible for a total of 139 jobs within the army; some women were trained as flight clerks. At its peak, the WAC contingent at New Castle numbered more than 425 members. (Delaware Public Archives, 1325.206, 633.)

RECRUITING THE WACS. As part of the recruiting effort for the WACs, this photograph was taken of a WAC being trained in the use of a machine gun. (Delaware Public Archives, 1325.206, 948–973.)

TRANSLATING FOR THE BOYS.
WAC Pfc. Iris Turillo (seated)
provided translation services
for Puerto Rican soldiers
stationed at the New Castle
Army Airbase. (Delaware Public
Archives, 1325.206, 605.)

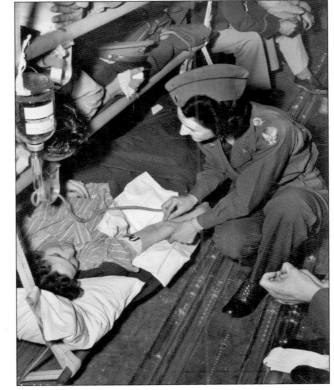

IN FLIGHT. Second Lt.
Ann Markowitz is shown
administering plasma to
an injured soldier being
air-lifted home. Providing
in-flight medical service was
a valuable role for women in
the military. (Delaware Public
Archives, 1325.206, 610.)

A Lighter Moment. Three members of the 552nd Army Airforce Base Unit at New Castle enjoy a lighter moment of relaxation at the base. Sgt. Jack Starkey plays the piano, while Privates First Class Salisbury and Krozsomski sing along. The civilian woman is identified as Jane Withers. (Delaware Public Archives, 1325.206, 533.)

Air Traffic Controller. An unidentified WAC serving as an air traffic controller at the New Castle Army Airbase maintains radio contact with aircraft from the tower. Air-traffic control was one of the vital functions staffed by women members of the service. (Delaware Public Archives, 1325.206, 616.)

WORKING THE LINE. Women workers, such as these at the Bellanca Aircraft Plant, provided an integral part of the war-related labor force in Delaware. Throughout the war, Bellanca produced gun turrets, planes, and other equipment for the Allied planes. (Delaware Public Archives, 1325.206, 2141.)

SIDE BY SIDE. Women workers lined up beside their male counterparts in many industries, including this team at Bellanca Aircraft, which was completing sub-assembly work on a bomber tail. (Delaware Public Archives, 1325.206, 2137.)

IT'S IN THE DETAILS. Allied aircraft required highly specialized and highly accurate work to be completed. At Bellanca, such requirements meant accurate filing of important fittings. (Delaware Public Archives, 1325.206, 2139.)

ASSEMBLY BENCH. Much of Bellanca's workforce toward the end of the war were women, who helped the company staff two production lines. This assembly bench was typical of the type of team-based work used at Bellanca. (Delaware Public Archives, 1325.206, 2069.)

MAKING GUN TURRETS. An entire line of women machine operators help to finish gun turrets manufactured at Bellanca Aircraft. By the end of the war, the company would be responsible for more than 35,000 such turrets. (Delaware Public Archives, 1325.205, box 1 chapter 20.)

DRILL PRESSES. Female employees at Bellanca work the drill presses. These women were among the 600 who worked at Bellanca and turned out more than 35,000 gun turrets. (Delaware Public Archives, 1325.205, 2141pn.)

ELBOW GREASE. This unidentified Bellanca worker puts a little extra effort into drilling holes in an aircraft assembly. (Delaware Public Archives, 1325.206, 2193.)

CRANE OPERATOR. Women did not shy from jobs on the assembly line, as attested to by this photograph of a woman operator on a 30-ton crane at the DuPont Company's Wilmington shops. It was not uncommon for women to step right into such roles traditionally held by men. (Delaware Public Archives, 1325.206, Box 1 Chapter 20.)

TRAIN CONDUCTOR. This unidentified conductor shows another role for women—staffing the transportation sector in Delaware. Women would assume roles as bus drivers, train lineman, and train conductors in order to support the war. (Delaware Public Archives, 1325.206, 2249.)

GIVING TWICE. These WACs show their support for the war in two ways—by serving as a member of the military and by donating to the United War Fund. (Delaware Public Archives, 1325.206, 2559.)

DRIVING THE TROLLEYS. These unidentified women stepped in to fill the void left by men leaving for the service and worked as trolley coach operators for the Delaware Coach Company in Wilmington. (Delaware Public Archives, 1325.205, box 1 chapter 20.)

SAVING HISTORY. Elizabeth Warren of the Wilmington Institute Free Library clips news of Delaware soldiers for preservation in the library's collection in 1942. Activities to preserve the history of Delaware's role in World War II—led by then State Archivist Leon deValinger Jr.—resulted in one of the richest collections of materials in the country. (Delaware Public Archives, 1325.206, 2979n.)

Four

"WILL YOU HELP?"
The American Red Cross and
Other Support Organizations

CHEMICAL WARFARE SERVICE. Soldiers of the Chemical Warfare Service are shown enjoying a hot meal provided by the Red Cross. The Delaware Chapter of the American Red Cross boasted over 15,000 volunteers during the war. The services the organization provided for the war effort were invaluable. (Delaware Public Archives, 1325.260, 2383.)

RED CROSS NURSING-GRAY LADIES. The Red Cross trained these women to assist nurses in hospitals, clinics, home health, and public health services. As a result, nurses were able to treat more patients. The first class was graduated in 1942. By 1945 there was an average of 145 Gray Ladies serving each month in Delaware. (Delaware Public Archives, 1325.206, 2434p.)

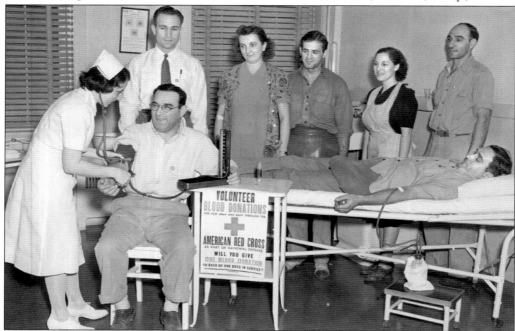

BLOOD DRIVE. Blood drives were a mainstay of the Red Cross efforts during the war. The Red Cross Plasma Bank first opened in Delaware on August 5, 1941, with 48 men and women volunteering a pint of blood. Three months later, a Dover effort was initiated at Kent General Hospital and 73 people donated blood. Incentives were established, including the "One Gallon Club" for those who donated a total of one gallon of blood. Henry McLane was the first to be recognized for this level of donation. (Delaware Public Archives, 1325.206, 2395p.)

RED CROSS WAR FUND DRIVE, 1943. The ladies of the Delaware Chapter of the American Red Cross are shown preparing for this important event. Pictured from left to right are (seated) Mrs. James T. Ward, Mrs. Stanley G. Ford, Mrs. Edward Blatz, Mrs. James M. Winfield (North Suburban Chairman), and Mrs. A.J. Northam; (standing) Mrs. Betty Walker, Mrs. W.H. Kiler, and Mrs. M.V. Boggs. (Delaware Public Archives, 1325.206, 2493.)

NURSING STUDENTS. A group of nursing students enjoy off hours at the Wilmington General Hospital. The nursing profession boomed during the war years, with the need for nurses reaching every part of the war effort, both at home and abroad. (Delaware Public Archives, 1325.206, 2442.)

WILL YOU HELP? These students at the Lore School—who served as junior Red Cross workers—are shown performing a variety of tasks for the war effort. The list on the wall shows what they have completed so far. This includes 900 Christmas cards for soldiers, 220 bookmarks, and 50 crossword puzzles. The poster on the wall asks the question posed to all Delawareans—"Will You Help?" (Delaware Public Archives, 1325.206, 1953p.)

RED CROSS CANTEEN. The canteen units provided fruit juices, coffee, doughnuts, and other refreshments at the New Castle, Fort Dupont, and Dover military bases. The most appreciated items were the refreshments served to the wounded who arrived in hospital planes at New Castle Air Base. In June 1945 there were 355 members in the Wilmington group and 155 in the Dover group. (Delaware Public Archives, 1325.206, 2384p.)

NUTRITION TIPS FROM UNCLE SAM. Two American Red Cross workers are shown working on a nutrition awareness program. Programs such as this one were also a good way of boosting morale on the home front. In the poster Uncle Sam declares "eat the right food daily." (Delaware Public Archives, 1325.206, 2438.)

NURSE CADETS ARRIVING FOR SCHOOL, C. 1940S. The war created a nursing shortage overseas and on the home front. Recruitment drives were held around the First State to help fill the need. (Delaware Public Archives, 1325.206,890.)

BUNDLES FOR BRITAIN, OCTOBER 24, 1941. (*above*) Workers from the British War Relief Society load needed supplies for overseas shipment. The campaign focused on supplying much needed goods to British civilians. (Delaware Public Archives, 1325.206, 2567.) (*below*) Students at the P.S. DuPont School gather supplies they collected for the Bundles for Britain Campaign. From left to right are Richard Bethards, treasurer, and Joanne Kurtz, chairwoman of the Social Service Committee. (Delaware Public Archives, 1325.206, 2568.)

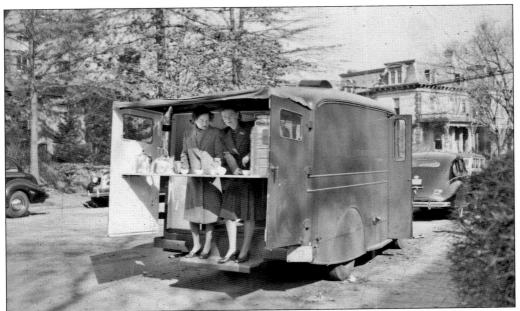

BRITISH FOOD CANTEEN "ROLLING KITCHEN," 1941. This mobile canteen was used by the British War Relief Society. All proceeds were used to purchase goods for needy British citizens. From left to right are Mrs. Petrus W. Turnbull and Mrs. Joel Turnbull. (Delaware Public Archives, 1325.206, 2561.)

SEWING UNIT, BRITISH WAR RELIEF SOCIETY HEADQUARTERS, WILMINGTON. The ladies are shown sewing some much needed clothes to help the allies in Britain. From left to right are Mrs. Thomas G Bradford, Mrs. Freeman C. Bishop, Mrs. Harcourt R. Burns, Mrs. Howard Duane, and Mrs. Floyd Kitchel. (Delaware Public Archives, 1325.206, 2573.)

BRITISH CHILDREN. Delawareans opened their homes to many displaced and refugee families from Europe. These British children are shown arriving in Wilmington, where they would spend the remainder of the war. (Delaware Public Archives, 1325.206, 1946.)

MAKING THE CLOTHES, BRITISH WAR RELIEF SOCIETY, JANUARY 31, 1942. Several members of the society are shown sewing clothes in the busy workroom. These clothes were made for children in Great Britain. From left to right are Mrs. Harcourt Burns, Mrs. Theodore Fletcher, and Mrs. Herbert Hunt. (Delaware Public Archives, 1325.206, 2570n.)

BRITISH WAR RELIEF AIDES. Knitting hats, scarves, and gloves for British citizens was a primary activity for these aides. From left to right are Mrs. William Prickett, Mrs. Ernest N. May, Mrs. George A. Elliott Jr., Mrs. Robert H. Richards Jr., and Mrs. Dudley Lunt. (Delaware Public Archives, 1325.206, 2571n.)

KNITTING FOR THE NEEDY, WILMINGTON. The British War Relief ladies are shown performing work on September 25, 1941. This organization was formed well before the United States became involved in the war. From left to right are Unit Chairman Mrs. Thomas G Bradford, Miss Mary Thornton, Miss Katherine Lee, Mrs. Harold Johnson, Miss Jesse M. Seaman, and Miss Isabelle B. Wales. (Delaware Public Archives, 1325.206, 2572n.)

ENGLISH FOXHOUNDS IN DELAWARE, FALL 1939. These prized English Foxhounds were actually war refugees from Great Britain. They were adopted by the Vicmead Hunt Club and received care for the duration of the war. (Delaware Public Archives, 1325.206, 2574n.)

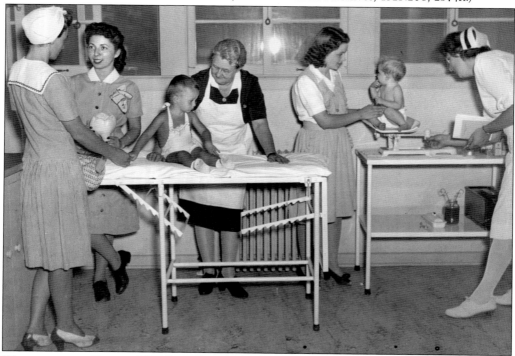

WEIGHING THE BABIES. The State Board of Health held "well child care" conferences several times a month, free of charge. From left to right are Mrs. Stanley Bird, Miss Hilda Bronfin (dental hygienist), Richard Bird (baby), Miss Tola Hastings (nurse), Mrs. Stanley Burgess with her baby, Patricia Ann, and Mrs. Grace Weiss (public health nurse). (Delaware Public Archives, 1325.206, 2050p.)

PICKING TOMATOES. Committee members of the Summer Food Relief Committee gather ripe tomatoes grown in the first state during the harvest in August 1942. The group was organized by the Wilmington Junior League, and provided food relief to those in need. From left to right are Mrs. George P. Bissel Jr. (chairman) and Mrs. Joseph A. Wheelock (vice chairman). (Delaware Public Archives, 1325.206, 2581n.)

GREEK WAR FUND RELIEF DRIVE, C. 1941. Frank Gregson, manager of the Hotel DuPont, is shown contributing funds raised at the hotel. From left to right are Mary Convas, Elsa Haldas, and Stella Garabicas. (Delaware Public Archives, 1325.206, 2578n.)

GRADUATION DAY,
DELAWARE HOSPITAL. These
nurses' aides are all smiles as
they participate in graduation
ceremonies. Nurses' aides
worked at a variety of facilities
in Delaware, including military
bases and civilian hospitals.
(Delaware Public Archives,
1325.205 Box 1, Chapter 17.)

NURSES' HONOR ROLL.
This honor roll of nurses was
organized by the American
Red Cross. (Delaware Public
Archives, 1325.206, 2450p.)

Five

"CANDY IS A FIGHTING FOOD"
The USO and the Home Front

DOVER USO CLUB GRAND OPENING, SEPTEMBER 9, 1943. This catchy slogan was used by the Dover USO Club at its grand opening on September 9, 1943 and appears on the pamphlet in the left corner of the picture. The overseas shipping boxes were stuffed with magazines, newspapers, books, and even a Delaware road map for servicemen to enjoy. (Delaware Public Archives, 1325.206, 2520.)

HALLOWEEN AT DOVER USO, c. 1940s. Doris Moore, junior hostess at the Dover USO, celebrates Halloween with an unidentified soldier. (Delaware Public Archives, 1325.206, 2552x.)

USO PARTY, DOVER. Soldiers and their families are shown enjoying the pleasant surroundings at the Dover USO. The jukebox in the rear of the picture was state-of-the-art in the 1940s. (1325.206, 2552qp.)

STRIKING UP THE BAND, USO DOVER. This band is shown entertaining soldiers and civilians during a weekend dance. Hundreds of dances were held at this location and were usually staffed by local volunteers. (Delaware Public Archives, 1325.206, 2552abp.)

USO CONCERT, REPAIR SHIP. Musician S.F. Greenwell of Wilmington entertains troops serving overseas. Such use of civilian talents was commonplace in the military during the war; service to the country was not limited in any way. (Delaware Public Archives, 1325.205, Box 1, Chapter 4.)

REST AND RELAXATION. (*above*) The USO Clubs provided recreation and entertainment to servicemen and their families. The clubs were located throughout the First State, including locations at Dover Army Air Base, Lewes, and Wilmington. A servicemen and some young ladies enjoy a game of checkers at a USO. (*below*) These soldiers enjoy a game of pool at the local USO.

CHRISTMAS 1944, USO CLUB. USO Clubs also provided respite and comfort for soldiers during the holiday season. These volunteers decorate a tree for soldiers; USO clubs would also provide holiday dinners and presents to men and women stationed in the community. (Delaware Public Archives, 1325.206, 137.)

REFRESHMENT STAND, TRAVELER'S AID USO. The Catholic Daughters of America were one in a long list of women's group that provided home front service to the nation. This USO stand was hosted by the Catholic Daughters of America, led by their chair, Mrs. E.F. Higgins. (Delaware Public Archives, 1325.206, 2542p.)

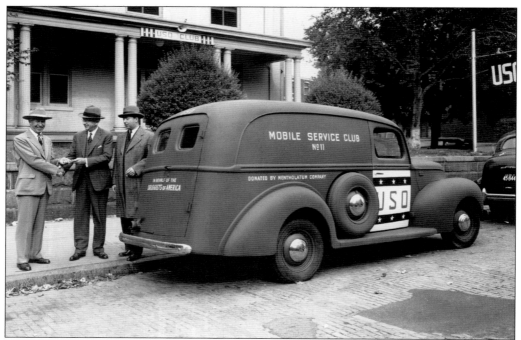

MOBILE SERVICE CLUB, C. 1940S. The Mobile Service Club was a program of the National Traveler's Aid Association, a wartime United Service Organization. Traveler's Aid staffed a USO station at the Wilmington railroad station; by war's end, more than 225,000 servicemen and women had used the facility. (Delaware Public Archives, 1325.206, 2525p.)

TRAVELER'S AID PARTY. The soldiers are shown at a dinner party sponsored by the Travelers Aid. This United Service Organization proved to be an invaluable source of help to soldiers and citizens during the war. (Delaware Public Archives, 1325.206, 2541p.)

IRONING HIS UNIFORM. Away from the comforts of home, this soldier tends to his laundry at a USO branch location. Simple comforts of laundry, food, and entertainment provided an invaluable morale boost to troops. (Delaware Public Archives, 1325.206, 2538p.)

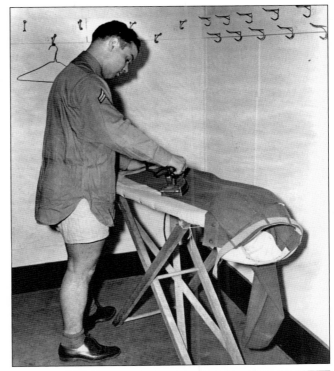

SPINNING RECORDS, TRAVELERS AID, USO. Two soldiers are seen chatting with some volunteers at a local USO function. This record player was state-of-the-art in the 1940s, providing music for numerous dances held at the facility. (Delaware Public Archives, 1325.206, 2535p.)

USO CHRISTMAS TOY CAMPAIGN, NOVEMBER 26, 1942. (*above*) These children are shown helping with this annual campaign at a local USO. The gifts would go to needy children in the area. Some of the toys collected include teddy bears, a bingo game, a movie starlets guide, and a little lady luncheon set. (Delaware Public Archives, 1325.206, 3222.) (*below*) Santa Claus was the guest of honor at the 1942 USO Christmas dinner. (Delaware Public Archives, 1325.206, 2695 pn.)

NEIGHBORHOOD SERVICE FLAGS DEDICATION, C. 1943. This "Marching to Victory" ceremony (see sign on flagpole) was held at 12th and West Streets. Many neighborhoods banded together around home front activities, including flag raising ceremonies such as this. (Delaware Public Archives, 1325.205, Box 1, chapter 17.)

SALVATION ARMY MOBILE CANTEEN. This mobile canteen was located at Front and Market Streets in Wilmington. (Delaware Public Archives, 1352.205, Box 1, Chapter 17.)

DELAWARE GIRL SCOUTS. The Girl Scouts are shown working during a salvage drive. Girl Scout troops across Delaware contributed greatly to salvage drives and Victory Gardens. (Delaware Public Archives, 1325.206, 3197p.)

DELAWARE GIRL SCOUTS TROOP 23, CHRISTMAS PREPARATION. The girl scouts were active in many programs to help the war effort. Some of these included Victory Gardens, salvage drives, and fund-raising efforts. The girls are shown preparing Christmas packages for overseas soldiers. (Delaware Public Archives, 1325.206, 1954p.)

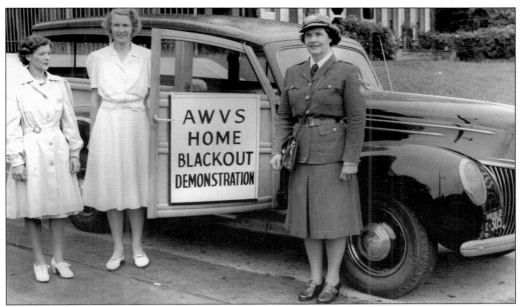

AWVS MOBILE BLACKOUT UNIT, JUNE 11, 1942. The American Women's Volunteer Service (AWVS) were called "the Molly Pitchers of the War," in reference to the invaluable service they performed. One such service helped the people of Wilmington prepare their homes for blackouts. From left to right are Mrs. Thomas A. Frazier, in charge of fingerprinting; Mrs. Charles F Richards, ARP instructor; and Mrs. Thomas Coyle, chairman of the AWVS Motor Corps. (Delaware Public Archives, 1325.206 Box 14.)

CHRISTMAS PRESENTS ON THE WAY. These presents would be sent to soldiers at Delaware State Hospital, New Castle Air Base, Fort DuPont, and Fort Miles. (Delaware Public Archives, 1325.206, 2587p.)

YARD OF DIMES DRIVE. This thermometer was used by the March of Dimes to raise money for infantile paralysis. Donors put dimes into the thermometer, which measured a yard. (Delaware Public Archives, 1325.206, 3198p.)

KENTMERE HONOR ROLL. Honor rolls such as this one in Kentmere were erected everywhere across Delaware and paid tribute to those who gave their lives in service to the country. Many such rolls exist still in the state. (Delaware Public Archives, 1325.206, 2592p.)

Six

"AMERICA CALLING"
Civilian Defense in Delaware

AMERICA CALLING. American Red Cross Workers are shown preparing bandages at the CD Center at 38th and Market Streets in Wilmington. The civilian defense sign reads, "America calling, take your place in civilian defense." Two signs in the background warn people not to talk about any activities important to the war effort. (Delaware Public Archives, 1325.205 Box 1.)

PENROSE STATION. The Penrose station was one of many such civilian defense stations opened across the state. Fort Miles in Lewes became the control center for the entire Delaware River and Bay defense system, including both military and civilian efforts. (Delaware Public Archives, 1325.206, 2001.)

CIVILIAN DEFENSE HEADQUARTERS, MILFORD. More than 100,000 Delawareans participated in civilian defense activities during the war. Local councils were set up to govern specific regions of the state. Some of the activities they performed daily were air-raid drills, evacuation plans, and airplane spotting. (Delaware Public Archives, 1325.205 Box 1.)

SPOTTING POST. There were 70 observation posts throughout the state, manned by civilian workers. These posts were manned each night to help spot enemy planes. Their warnings would be passed down the chain of command to Air Raid Wardens, Sectors and Block Captains. At the peak, there were 8,900 volunteer spotters and 15,000 to 20,000 volunteer Wardens, Sectors, and Block Captains. (Delaware Public Archives, 1325.205 Box 1.)

AIRPLANE SPOTTER. This female airplane spotter was on duty at the U.S. Army Air Corps observation post in Arden on February 21, 1942. (Delaware Public Archives, 1325.206, 1967.)

CIVILIAN DEFENSE WORKERS. These members of the Junior Civilian Defense group sold tags to support the Coast Guard Center. (Delaware Public Archives, 1325.206, 2010p.)

WOMEN FIRE INSPECTORS. Although faced with a severe shortage of volunteers, Delaware's strong and proud volunteer fire service met the challenge of provided fire protection throughout the war. Women stepped in to serve roles in support of the fire service, as evidenced by these fire inspectors. (Delaware Public Archives, 1325.206, 2005.)

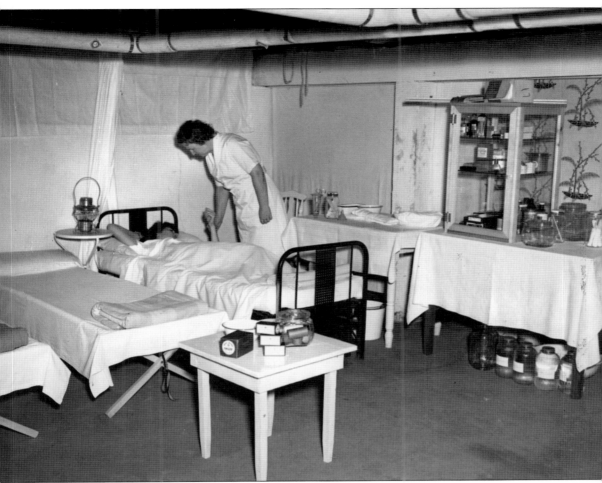

Dressing Station, Elsmere, New Castle County, 1942. These stations were set up in private residences and were designed to treat local civilians in case of enemy attack. The location pictured is the home of Mrs. Theodore Jack, who is shown posing as a nurse. Mrs. J.W. Hoffa is posing as the injured patient. For more serious injuries, 22 casualty stations were set up throughout the county. (Delaware Public Archives, 1325.206, 2019.)

OFFICE OF CIVILIAN DEFENSE, MUNICIPAL BUILDING, WILMINGTON. This office was a major hub of activity for civilian defense efforts in the First State. Some of the many activities the group oversaw were the Aircraft Warning Service, the Victory Gardens, the Airplane Spotters, and the Disaster Squads. (Delaware Public Archives, 1325.206, 2003p.)

TELEPHONE DISPATCH. The telephone dispatch crew is pictured at the Air Raid Warning Center in New Castle. These dispatch crews enacted "phone trees" to alert those residents who had phone service of possible attacks or drills. Involving citizens in military-based operations required a level of sensitivity and security, as evidenced by the sign on the wall (upper left), which reads, "What you do here, What you see here, What you say here, When you leave here, Let it stay here." (Delaware Public Archives, 1325.206, 2202.)

Seven

"Scrap Is Our Goal"
Saving and Salvaging to Support the War

Scrap is Our Goal. Students from Bayard Junior High School join other students from Delaware is raising the awareness of scrap drives. Such efforts to conserve and re-use such everyday items as paper, wood, and metal resulted in huge savings to the country, and were part of community-wide events. Bayard Junior High School collected more than 7,000 unwanted keys, with student Daphne Powell responsible for bringing in more than 1,000 keys alone. (Delaware Public Archives, 1325.206, 2306pn.)

PAPER DRIVE. The Boy Scouts of Lewes conducted a paper drive as part of their community service. The truckloads of paper included newspaper from homes, but also unwanted records, packing material, and cardboard from businesses. (Delaware Public Archives, 1325.205, Box 1 Chapter 17.)

SCOUTS HONOR. This scrap paper drive was only one example of the meritorious and honorable service the Boy Scouts played in home front activities. Scrap drives were not a one-time occurrence, and many Boy Scouts volunteered weekly to gather items and transport them to central collection locations. (Delaware Public Archives, 1325.206, 2303.)

WILMINGTON BOY SCOUTS. Boy Scouts throughout the state did more than just scrap drives. Throughout the war, many Boy Scouts left their homes for the summer months to work on the farms in southern Delaware—which were depleted of workers—ensuring that the harvest was completed on time. These Wilmington Boy Scouts are shown receiving final instructions at the foot of Wilmington's Caesar Rodney statue before embarking on another drive. (Delaware Public Archives, 1325.206, 2583p.)

HEAVY LOAD, OCTOBER 1942. A group of children are shown pulling—or attempting to pull—their wagon packed with salvageable materials. In January 1942 the National War Production Board established a war mobilization program whose chief function was salvage operations. In Delaware, this was carried out by the Delaware State Salvage Committee. (Delaware Public Archives, 1325.206, 2309pn.)

WOODEN BUMPER, 1942. This young Delawarean's sacrifice was easy to see: a wooden bumper on her car. Her metal bumper was sent to a collection point to be melted down. (Delaware Public Archives, 1325.206, 2333 pn.)

ALL SCRAP IS GOOD SCRAP. These young men show ingenuity by removing an out-of-date pulley and sending it to the salvage drive. When it came to salvage drives, everything was possible: even household cooking fat was salvaged for the glycerin content and later re-used in the making of explosives. (Delaware Public Archives, 1325.206, 2310 pn.)

BILLY EVANS. A young Billy Evans turns in old rubber at the L.E. Wadman filling station at 1603 Pennsylvania Avenue in Wilmington on June 15, 1942. The poster on the right includes of picture of soldiers in a jeep, with the exclamation "They've got more important places to go than you!" (Delaware Public Archives, 1325.206, 2336.)

HEAVY LIFTING. Even the youngest Delawareans helped the salvage drives, as evidenced by these two youngsters carrying a section of pipe. (Delaware Public Archives, 1325.206, 2313pn.)

GAS RATIONING. These cars are shown lining up for gas on December 18, 1942, just before gas sales and prices across Delaware were "frozen" by the Office of Price Administration. The OPA controlled prices of commodities throughout Delaware to avoid inflation and provide stable pricing. (Delaware Public Archives, 1325.206, 2280.)

CLOTHING DRIVES. Clothing drives were conducted across Delaware and repaired clothes were then re-distributed in the state. As the war continued, many of the clothes collected were sent overseas to help displaced persons and refugees. (Delaware Public Archives, 1325.206, 2297.)

TIN MAN. Among the oddest finds in all of the scrap drives was this replica of the "tin man" replete with a suit of armor and weaponry. (Delaware Public Archives, 1325.206, 2330pn.)

A MOUNTAIN OF SCRAP. These students add to a growing mountain of scrap of industrial waste. The efforts of the State Salvage Committee resulted in a total of 30 tons of materials being salvaged throughout the state. (Delaware Public Archives, 1325.206, 2307pn.)

A Wagon Full. These children used wagons, trolleys, carts, and anything with wheels to bring their scrap to their school's salvage drive. (Delaware Public Archives, 1325.206, 2305pn.)

Sallies Help Out. These Salesianum Academy students—known more commonly as "Sallies"—did their part by piling up the scrap at the corner of West 8th Street and West Street in Wilmington. (Delaware Public Archives, 1325.206, 2314pn.)

Eight

"THE JOB HAS BEEN DONE"
Feeding the War

THE JOB HAS BEEN DONE. One of the consequences of so many men serving overseas was the shortage of farm labor to harvest crops grown across Delaware. The job of ensuring the harvest was organized by the Delaware Emergency Farm Labor Program, and included the use of school children, Boy Scouts, and Girl Scouts to pick crops. Thanks to the efforts of these and other citizens, the harvests of both 1943 and 1944 were completed without any crop loss—and achievement boasted of in the annual report of the Emergency Farm Labor Program when they said "The job has been done." (Delaware Public Archives, 1325.205, box 1 chapter 19.)

PLOWING THE FIELDS, C. 1940s. These city school children worked under the Delaware Victory Farm Volunteer Program. Some of the products they harvested included corn, tomatoes, soybeans, and apples. (Delaware Public Archives, 1325.205, Box 1, Chapter 19.)

VICTORY GARDEN. This Victory Garden was planted and maintained by Boy Scout Troop 49 on Delaware Avenue in Wilmington; it included cabbages, tomatoes, and beans. Victory Gardens grew across the state as part of a concerted effort to provide food and to conserve such items as rubber and gasoline. Mrs. William S. Dutton of Wilmington chaired the Victory Garden Committee and the program included gardens started by 4-H Clubs, Boy and Girl Scouts, Future Farmers of America, and schools. (Delaware Public Archives, 1325.205, 1938.)

CoolSpring Farm Labor Camp Workers, 1943. Several workers emigrated from the Bahamas and worked the harvest in 1943. This labor camp was located in Sussex County and was staffed by over 95 Bahamians. The men were recruited by the County Farm Labor Advisory Committee. Another labor camp was set up at Woodside. These workers helped ease the burden put on Delaware farmers during the war. (Delaware Public Archives, 1325.205, Box 1, Chapter 19.)

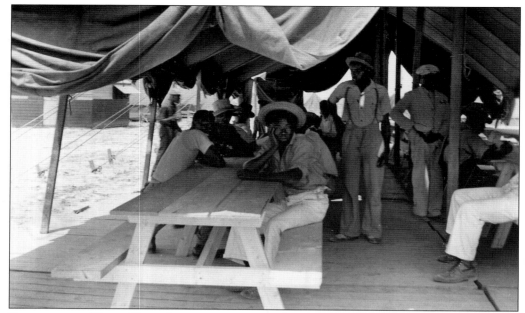

BEATING THE HEAT. These Jamaican emergency farm workers at the Woodside Labor Camp take a break on a long hot summer day in 1943. Two camps were set up in 1943 to accommodate the influx of foreign workers, who were recruited to help with the farm labor shortage. This camp was located just outside of Dover. (Delaware Public Archives, 1325.206, 1930p.)

JAMAICANS AT WOODSIDE, SUMMER 1943. Several Jamaican workers prepare for a day in the fields. Their efforts greatly helped Delaware farm production and the allied war effort. (Delaware Public Archives, 1325.206, 1929p.)

FORT MILES SOLDIERS TENDING THE FIELDS. These Fort Miles soldiers share a light moment on a picturesque summer day. Soldiers were often recruited when crops became in danger of not being picked in time. Many Fort Miles soldiers helped rescue crops at farms around the state. (RG 1325.205 Box 1, Chapter 19.)

SCHOOL CHILDREN IN THE FIELDS, c. 1940s. The children are shown hard at work helping to harvest the crop. Victory Farm Volunteers were heavily recruited around the state. Some of the volunteers working downstate were offered room and board with farm families during the summer season. (Delaware Public Archives, 1325.205, 1922p.)

VFW Farm Labor Camp, Bridgeville. This camp housed over 50 Boy Scouts during the summer of 1943. The Delmarva Council of Boy Scouts were heavily involved in recruitment for the Victory Gardens programs. The boy scouts also assisted in blood and scrap drives to help in the war effort. (Delaware Public Archives, 1325.206, 1928.)

Working the Fields. Two schoolboys are shown working the fields, part of the effort to use children from Northern Delaware to assist in the harvest In the front is Harry Moore of Minquadale School, and in the back is Clifford Murphy of A.I. DuPont School. (Delaware Public Archives, 1325.206, 1925.)

VICTORY GARDEN, P.S. DUPONT SCHOOL, 1944. Students are shown working on their garden at this Wilmington school. The gardens helped drum up morale on the home front, allowing many Delawareans to use their backyards to assist the war effort. These gardens helped ease the labor and food production shortage Delaware experienced during the 1940s. (Delaware Public Archives, 1325.205, Box 1, Chapter 19.)

VICTORY GARDEN DISPLAY. Victory Garden harvest shows were held in the fall of each year. The best crops from selected Victory Gardens were put on display. The shows included several contests designed to boost morale and grow bigger crops. Many prizes and authentic certificates were given to winners throughout the state. (Delaware Public Archives, 1325.206, 1937.)

PICKING STRAWBERRIES NEAR BRIDGEVILLE. Alberta Pardham is shown gathering the strawberry crop for harvest. Due to the farm labor shortage, women and girls were often recruited to volunteer when the harvest drew near. Special day camps were set up in close proximity to Wilmington and allowed thousands of area children to work on nearby farms. (Delaware Public Archives, 1325.206, 1923p.)

PLANTING THE CROP, C. 1943. During the war, parts were scarce to fix machinery. Many farmers continued on the old-fashioned way, with a mule and buggy. (Delaware Public Archives, 1325.206, 1931p.)

Nine

A Soldier's Life

DRAFT TRAIN. Draft inductees are seen leaving on a train in Wilmington in 1940. This crowded scene would be repeated, again and again, as young soldiers and their families packed train platforms before being deployed across the country and across the world. (Delaware Public Archives, 1325.206, 1532.)

TAKING THE OATH. Maj. Frank T. Lynch of the U.S. Army Recruiting Service in Wilmington instructs young enlistees from the Wilmington area. Delaware would boast more than 33,000 soldiers who served during the war. (Delaware Public Archives, 1325.205, box 1 chapter 15.)

INSPECTING THE TROOPS. Gov. Walter W. Bacon reviews the troops at Fort DuPont on November 21, 1941. Bacon served as governor from 1941 to 1949, overseeing the home front efforts of Delaware throughout the war, and then transitioning the state to the post-war economy. (Delaware Public Archives, 1325.205, 734.)

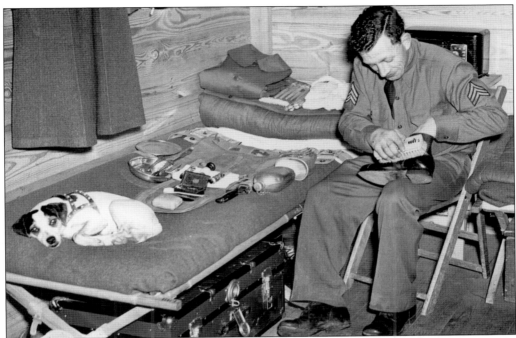

SHOE SHINE. An unidentified sergeant shines his boots in the barracks at Fort DuPont amidst the common allotment of gear for a soldier: a cot, a foot locker, blankets, pillow, uniform, and a canteen. Two additions to the usual gear include a radio—which can be seen just behind the sergeant—and a dog. (Delaware Public Archives, 1325.206, 1445.)

GETTING READY FOR KICK-OFF. One of the regular features of stateside postings—in addition to military duty—was the ability to engage in sports and other recreational activities. Fort DuPont was similar to many other military posts across the United States, accepting soldiers who were either training for deployment overseas, or housing soldiers who performed home front security. This November 1941 game between Fort DuPont and the Wilmington Clippers, a semi-professional football team, was well attended, with proceeds going to the purchase of Fort DuPont team uniforms. (Delaware Public Archives, 1325.206, 756p.)

FORT DUPONT BAND. Bands such as these served two purposes—they provided entertainment for soldiers and also provided for community outreach activities. (Delaware Public Archives, 1325.206, 749pn.)

THE SANDUNAIRS. The Sandunairs, an all-military dance band, pose prior to a dance at the Fort Miles post theater. Bi-monthly dances were held on the post to boost the morale of the stationed troops. (Delaware Public Archives, 1325.205, Box 1 Chapter 3.)

BOXING MATCH. This 1943 boxing match at Fort DuPont was part recreation and part training, as soldiers used the opportunity to practice basic hand-to-hand combat skills. Civilians were welcome to these impromptu matches, as evidenced by the small boy with his bicycle on the right. (Delaware Public Archives, 1325.206, 754p.)

GOLF TOURNAMENT. Col. George Ruhler, commanding officer of Fort DuPont, plays a practice round of golf with some enlisted men. The men were preparing for a benefit golf tournament to be held at Wilmington County Club, which raised money for the Education and Recreation Fund at Fort DuPont. (Delaware Public Archives, 1325.206, 757p.)

HANDS ON HIPS, READY FOR ACTION. Unidentified Fort Miles soldiers were part of a comedy skit held by the USO. While it was not uncommon to hold such skits, it is safe to assume that the uniforms on these men were uncommon. (Delaware Public Archives, 1325.206, 839pn.)

ROLLEN ABROAD. Another example of theatrical presentation, *Rollen Abroad* was performed by the men of Fort Miles in December 1943. Those pictured include Sgt. Mark Laub, Sgt. Jesse Berman, Chief Warrant Officer Henry K. Schmidt, and Cpl. David Fitzgibbon at the piano. Standing (left to right) are Pfc. Joseph McComiskey, Cpl. Joseph Scwarzman, Sgt. Edward Lalent, Pvt. William Walker, Pvt. Harry Donlevy, Cpl. Charles Lewis, Cpl. Thomas Willem, Pfc. John Fox, Sgt. Ben Chambellan, Pfc. Craig Edwards, Pvt. James Lyre, and Pvt. Fred Balliger. (Delaware Public Archives, 1325.206, 837p.)

WAITING FOR THE BELL. Standing at attention during the playing of the National Anthem, soldiers and civilians alike await the start of an afternoon of boxing at Fort Miles. (Delaware Public Archives, 1325.206, 842 pn.)

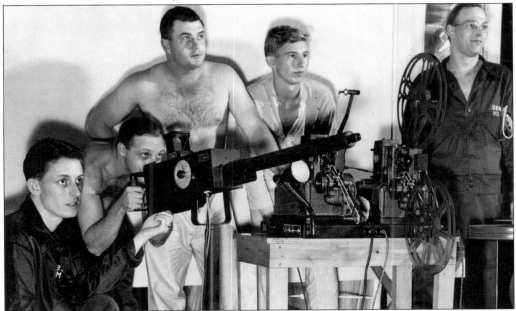

WOUNDED GUNNERS. Wounded soldiers recovering at the New Castle Army Air Base are trained in gunnery during their convalescence. Training exercises for the men included the use of films (see projector at right) and gun sites used on training guns. (Delaware Public Archives, 1325.206, 663p.)

WOUNDED ARRIVE AT NEW CASTLE. Wounded soldiers arrive at the New Castle Army Air Base after returning from Europe. (Delaware Public Archives, 1325.205, Box 1 Chapter 3.)

OPEN HOUSE. An open house at the New Castle Army Air Base attracted hundreds of local residents, who were able to tour military planes and vehicles. Open house events such as these were used to build local support for the base. (Delaware Public Archives, 1325.206, 495.)

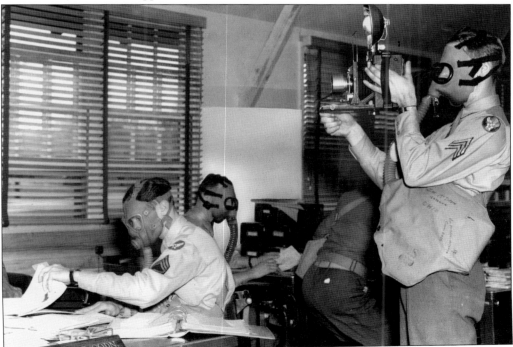

GAS MASK DRILL. A gas mask drill is conducted at the New Castle Army Air Base. Such drills became a regular part of training for many state-side troops. (Delaware Public Archives, 1325.206, 669p.)

OPENING DAY, 1944. Opening day for the New Castle Army Air Base baseball team included the ceremonial first pitch being thrown out by the (unidentified) presiding officer. Others in the picture include Lieutenant Hoskins, Mace Nowell, Lieutenant Martin, Capt. Stan Keller, and Joe DeMarco. (Delaware Public Archives, 1325.206, 565p.)

NEW CASTLE CAGERS. This basketball team from the New Castle Army Air Base played teams throughout the area. Because of redeployment of personnel throughout their season, the team often had new players. (Delaware Public Archives, 1325.206, 574p.)

WRESTLING MOVES. Another recreational outlet that doubled as training was wrestling. These instructors are shown demonstrating a single-arm takedown as the men look on. (Delaware Public Archives, 1325.206, 579p.)

TUTU. These soldiers receive some last minute instructions on an upcoming theatrical performance. (Delaware Public Archives, 1325.206, 584p.)

PHILADELPHIA ATHLETICS. Members of the Philadelphia Athletics visit with enlisted men and women from Delaware after one of their home games in Philadelphia. Athletics players include, from left to right, Earl Brucker, George Kell, Al Simmons, and Earl Mack. (Delaware Public Archives, 1325.206, 567p.)

MASCOT. The mascot at New Castle Army Air Base—a goat—receives a drink of milk from one of his caretakers. Mascots were common as units sought to build both identity and morale on base. (Delaware Public Archives, 1325.206, 468p.)

SPORTS SHOW AT NEW CASTLE. Local women sell tickets for "The Weekend of Sports" show held at the New Castle Army Air Base. The show included an appearance by New York Yankee Joe DiMaggio, and all proceeds went to supporting the entertainment and recreation of those serving on the base. (Delaware Public Archives, 1325.206, 532p.)

THE GRAND BALL. The Grand Ball held at the New Castle Army Air Base in June 1944 attracted hundreds of soldiers and local residents who marked the second anniversary of the base. (Delaware Public Archives, 1325.206, 545p.)

CHRISTMAS DANCE, 1943. The Christmas Dance at the Dover Army Air Base was a regular feature of life on the base. Sponsored by the USO, the dance provided a welcome diversion for those men and women who would be away from their families for the holidays. (Delaware Public Archives, 1325.206, 176.)

P-47s. The Dover Army Air Field was home to the P-47 Thunderbolts and served as a vital training ground for many Army pilots being trained on this state of the art fighter. (Delaware Public Archives, 1325.205, Box 1 Chapter 3.)

WAR DOG TRAINING. War dog training at the Dover Army Air Field included an obstacle course for the dogs. (Delaware Public Archives, 1325.206, 222.)

KENNELS AT DOVER. Dogs were trained for a variety of purposes, including detection of explosives. (Delaware Public Archives, 1325.206, 223.)

THE ANDREWS SISTERS. The caption on this photo says it all: "Soldiers at the Dover Army Air Field presented the musical revue 'DAAFie Delights' for the citizens of Dover with the highlight being the comic impersonation of the Andrews Sisters by these three privates, left to right: Paul Costello of Scranton, PA; Joseph J. McPhieters of San Francisco; and Albert Rodman of Brooklyn, NY." (Delaware Public Archives, 1325.206, 134.)

CAUGHT IN THE ACTION. A serviceman "cuts the rug" with a local Dover girl during a dance at the Dover Army Air Field in September 1944. (Delaware Public Archives, 1325.206, 168.)

DOVER OPEN HOUSE. Residents of Dover climb all over a fighter plane as part of an open house held at the base. Two young boys at the left are shown attempting to climb onto the wing of the plane. (Delaware Public Archives, 1325.206, 150.)

SOLDIERS VOTE, TOO. Soldiers at the Dover Army Air Field receive their voting application cards. In order to vote in elections, soldiers obtained absentee ballots, a practice which is still in place today. (Delaware Public Archives, 1325.206, 132.)

BATTER UP. This unidentified soldier readies a pitch for the Dover Army Air Field team. Similar to other teams at Fort DuPont, the Dover team played a mix of games between other base teams as well as local teams. (Delaware Public Archives, 1325.206, 184-201.)

DOVER CAGERS. The Dover basketball team poses for a picture prior to playing in the 1944 season. (Delaware Public Archives, 1325.206, 184–201.)

SAFE. A player slides safely into home during at game at the Dover Army Air Base. (Delaware Pubic Archives, 1325.206, 184–201.)

312TH SQUADRON. The 312th squadron team poses prior to playing a game at the Dover Army Air Field. (Delaware Public Archives, 1325.206, 184–201.)

DIAMOND STATE TANKER. Gov. Elbert "Bert" Carvel and Staff Sergeant Goodin christen the *Diamond State Tanker* at the Dover Army Air Field on Armed Forces Day. The naming of planes for Delaware was recently renewed, when a C-5 was re-named *Spirit of the Blue Hen*. (Delaware Public Archives, 1325.206, 202-223.)

SENDING PACKAGES. These servicemen send home packages from the Dover Army Air Base post office. Maintaining postal service to the men and women in the service was a vital function of bases like New Castle and Dover. (Delaware Public Archives, 1325.206, 127–145.)

Ten

I HEREBY SURRENDER
Prisoners of War Held in Delaware

I HEREBY SURRENDER. The 21-member crew of the German U-858 submarine, appearing worried and apprehensive, arrives at Fort Miles in Lewes on May 14, 1945, just after the formal surrender of their vessel. Afloat in the waters off the coast of Newfoundland upon the surrender of Germany, the sub flew a black flag, per the armistice agreement, signifying that it was permitting the U.S. Marines to board. The sub, with its crew, was then towed to the mouth of the Delaware Bay, just across from Cape May, New Jersey. It was here that the Lt. Thilo Bode formally surrendered the submarine. The U-858 was the first enemy submarine to surrender to the Allies after the armistice. (Delaware Public Archives, 1325.206, 847.)

AT THE MOMENT OF BOARDING. The event of the surrender was well documented by U.S. Navy photographers. This photo shows the sub at the moment of boarding by U.S. Marines. The submarine was responsible for the sinking of 16 Allied ships. (Delaware Public Archives, 1325.206, 843.)

ON ALLIED SOIL. The crew of the U-858 sub takes its first steps on Allied soil, as they land at Fort Miles. Their next hours would be spent being searched and transported to prison barracks. (Delaware Public Archives, 1325.206,854.)

DEFEATED. Lieutenant Thilo Bode, the 27-year old captain of the captured U-858 submarine, has an Allied-supplied cigarette while awaiting further instruction. Bode's scowl at the photographer provides a clear portrait of his feelings about the surrender. (Delaware Public Archives, 1325.206, 844.)

TRANSPORTING THE PRISONERS. Once the surrender of the submarine took place, the German prisoners were placed on a small transport ship for their journey to Fort Miles. U.S. Soldiers provided each of the German prisoners with an "Emergency Seaman Kit" provided by the Red Cross. (Delaware Public Archives, 1325.206, 845.)

STANDING ROOM ONLY. The prisoners are packed into the rear of a small transport boat that will dock in a few short moments. With looks ranging from bewilderment to relief, the German prisoners await the landing on Allied soil. (Delaware Public Archives, 1325.206, 851.)

CLIMBING OFF. The prisoners climb off the transport ship and onto the dock in Lewes. (Delaware Public Archives, 1325.206, 853.)

210 PRISONERS; 210 SEARCHES. The searching of all 210 crew members was meticulous, including their possessions and all of their gear. (Delaware Public Archives, 1325.206, 858.)

SIDEARM SURRENDERED. This German prisoner surrenders his sidearm to his Allied captor. (Delaware Public Archives, 1325.206, 859.)

SEARCHING THE PRISONERS. The search of prisoners included every person, bag, and every piece of clothing. (Delaware Public Archives, 1325.206, 860.)

PREVENTING SABOTAGE. In addition to the search of individuals for contraband, the submarine stayed in the Delaware Bay for two days while it was searched for signs of sabotage. (Delaware Public Archives, 1325.206, 861.)

FINAL INSTRUCTIONS. Once searched, prisoners were given instructions, in German, through an interpreter, on where they would be held. (Delaware Public Archives, 1325.206, 856.)

HEADING FOR PRISON. The German prisoners are marched down the pier toward awaiting trucks for their transport to prison barracks. (Delaware Public Archives, 1325.206, 855.)

A TRUCKLOAD OF PRISONERS. Packed shoulder-to-shoulder, the prisoners are transported by truck to the barracks. (Delaware Public Archives, 1325.206, 865.)

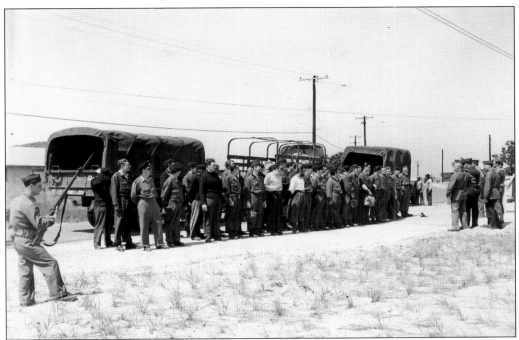

PRISON RULES. With armed sentries standing within sight, the German prisoners arrived at the prison barracks and are read a series of rules about the next phase of imprisonment. (Delaware Public Archives, 1325.206, 864.)

SEARCHING SOCKS. The prisoners were issued prison uniforms and their German uniforms were then searched, again, for any signs of contraband. (Delaware Public Archives, 1325.206, 869.)

INTO THE BARRACKS. The German prisoners reach the next destination in their military service—an Allied prison barracks. (Delaware Public Archives, 1325.206, 868.)

FIRST MEAL. The mess kitchen at Fort Miles serves the German prisoners their first meal after arrival. The kitchen was re-fitted with German signage, which detailed the rules of the mess. (Delaware Public Archives, 1325.206, 870.)

WORK DETAIL. With shovels in hand and a large "P" on their clothes, these POWs head to work detail at Fort DuPont, which housed more than 1,000 German POWs. At the peak of POW activity in 1945, more than 4,000 POWs were held in Delaware and worked in such industries as poultry processing, orchard work, crop picking, and package manufacturing. POWs worked in such towns as Georgetown, Leipsic, Lewes, Harrington, Bethany Beach, and Bridgeville; it was reported that the use of Nazi prisoners in the state had resulted in more than $2,400,000 in payments for the labor. (Delaware Public Archives, 1325.205, box 1 chapter 3.)

A MORE RELAXING MOMENT. After acclimating to prison life, it was reported that many prisoners enjoyed their time in Delaware and preferred the climate and work to what awaited them in Germany. (Delaware Public Archives, 1325.206, 809.)

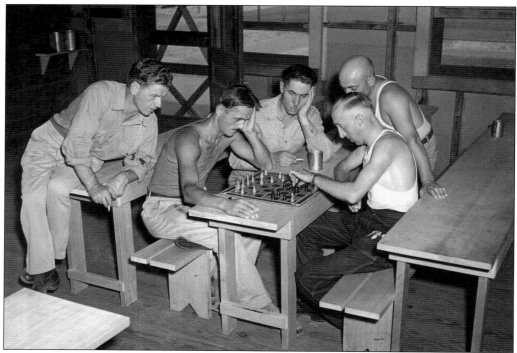

FORT DUPONT CHESS GAME. Some prisoners played chess to pass their internment at Fort DuPont. (Delaware Public Archives, 1325.206, 807.)

TUNING IN THE RADIO. Prisoners at Fort DuPont were afforded the luxury of a radio on occasion, allowing them to keep abreast of developments overseas. (Delaware Public Archives, 1325.206, 806.)

Eleven

ONE NATION, ONE CAUSE
Celebrating Victory

MARCHING IN WILMINGTON. Fort DuPont soldiers march in Wilmington during the 1941 Memorial Day parades. Holidays and parades took on a different role during war, providing soldiers with the ability to proudly show their expertise and providing civilians with an opportunity to thank those in service. The single cause of World War II united the country and Delaware. (Delaware Public Archives, 1325.205, box 1 chapter 3.)

MEMORIAL DAY, 1943. As the war grinded on, public displays of patriotism grew in frequency and in size. This Memorial Day parade in 1943 shows streets lined citizens showing their support for the country. (Delaware Public Archives, 1325.206, 2670n.)

ALLIED FLAGS. The dedication of the flags of the Allied Nations on Rodney Square in Wilmington drew thousands of spectators. The show of unity for the Allied cause—flying the flags of all nations fighting for the Allies—would continue on Rodney Square throughout the war. (Delaware Public Archives, 1325.205, box 1 chapter 17.)

MARCHING IN DELAWARE CITY. Fort DuPont soldiers dominate the streetscape in Delaware City on Memorial Day, 1943. (Delaware Public Archives, 1325.205, box 1 chapter 3.)

V-E CELEBRATION. As news of the victory over the Axis forces reached Wilmington on May 8, 1945, paper was dumped out of windows and crowds gathered on the street. This poignant photograph—taken the corner of 10th and Market Streets in Wilmington, just outside the Wilmington Trust Building—captures the competing emotions of the day: citizens celebrate a victory, while a serviceman makes his way back to duty. News of the victory, while a relief for many serviceman, meant that they would be re-deployed to other duty in support of the war fronts opened in Asia. (Delaware Public Archives, 1325.206, 2619.)

V-J CELEBRATION, 5:00 P.M. News of the Allied victory over the Axis reached many people during the work day. Offices stopped their work and filled the sky with scrap paper and confetti in celebration. This photograph of the corner of 11th and Orange taken at 5:00 p.m., as workers were leaving their buildings, shows the results of the celebration. (Delaware Public Archives, 1325.206, 2622p.)

V-J CELEBRATION, 7:15 P.M., 10TH AND MARKET STREETS. This picture was taken on August 14, 1945, just moments after the announcement of victory over Japan and the end of the war. This was normally a calm time of day for Wilmington, but the sequence of photographs depicts how a summer evening was transformed into a celebration—an event that occurred across the state. (Delaware Public Archives, 1325.206, 2621p.)

V-J Celebration, 7:30 p.m., 10th and Market Streets. Taken 15 minutes later, this photograph from the same location gives a sense of the milling crowds. A police officer, hands on hips, stands by to ensure the safety of the celebration, which now includes all ages. A young boy, with a wide smile, is seen running across the street (in the lower middle of the photograph), no doubt creating a memory that would last his lifetime. (Delaware Public Archives, 1325.206, 2620pn.)

V-J Celebration, 7:45 p.m., 10th and Market Streets. The crowds grew exponentially after the dinner hour, as young and old alike celebrated the end of a war that changed each of their lives. This photograph provides some irony: on the right-hand side is a woman taking photographs with her Brownie camera. Somewhere among a Delawarean's personal archives is a picture of this same scene, taken by her. (Delaware Public Archives, 1325.206, 2625pn.)

V-J CELEBRATION, 7:45 P.M. 10TH AND MARKET STREETS. A final shot by our unidentified photographer reflects the entire story of Delaware's home front support of the war—male and female, young and old, all united. (Delaware Public Archives, 1325.206, 2626p.)

GOING HOME. On October 15, 1945, the fist discharged soldiers from the separation center at Fort Miles leave their post and head home. Delawareans continued to show their support for these brave men and women with welcome home parties and, more importantly, with jobs in the new post-war economy. (Delaware Public Archives, 1325.206, 53.)

A Word on Chapter Titles

Many of the chapter titles in this volume are drawn from slogans used during the war. These slogans appeared in advertisements, on posters, and on letterhead and were created to boost morale and encourage broad participation in the home front activities.

"We Need You Now" appears in a recruiting poster on page 9. The poster was used to attract new workers to war-related industries.

"Block Out This Menace" was the slogan that towered over Wilmington as part of a drive to sell war bonds. The poster appears on page 21.

"Are You a Girl With a Star-Spangled Heart?" appears in a recruiting poster for the Women's Air Corp; the poster is seen hanging on the wall in the photograph on page 31.

"Will You Help?" was the question put to students and adults alike by the American Red Cross. Junior Red Cross students at Lore School read the question everyday on the poster that hung in their classroom; that poster appears on page 46.

"Candy is Fighting Food Too" was a slogan used to get donations to support the troops. The poster it appears on is on page 55.

"America Calling" was a creative slogan used to highlight the use of telephones by the Civilian Defense to notify neighborhoods of potential attacks and drills. The poster appears on page 67.

"Scrap is Our Goal" is the bold banner carried by students from the Bayard Junior High School on page 73.

"The Job Has Been Done" was a proclamation by a state official declaring that no crops were lost as a result of the shortage of farm labor during harvest time. The statement was both a proclamation and a message of congratulations to the many people who assisted in the effort.

Three chapter titles are drawn from another source: the authors' interpretation of images and the unspoken slogans, which were apparent. "A Soldier's Life" was meant to depict the soldier's life in Delaware, where many soldiers received a welcome respite from the brutalities of the war. "I Hereby Surrender" typifies many of the compelling photographs of German prisoners of war as they face their first moments on enemy soil as surrendered prisoners. Finally, "One Nation, One Cause" sums up the faces of so many Delawareans who appear in the photographs of V-E and V-J Day celebrations.